Picture the Past
SCHOOL

Jane Shuter

Heinemann
LIBRARY

First published in Great Britain by Heinemann Library
Halley Court, Jordan Hill, Oxford OX2 8EJ
a division of Reed Educational & Professional Publishing Ltd

OXFORD FLORENCE PRAGUE MADRID ATHENS
MELBOURNE AUCKLAND KUALA LUMPUR SINGAPORE TOKYO
IBADAN NAIROBI KAMPALA JOHANNESBURG GABORONE
PORTSMOUTH NH (USA) CHICAGO MEXICO CITY SAO PAULO

Designed by Ken Vail Graphic Design, Cambridge
Colour separations by Dot Gradations, Wickford, Essex
Printed in Malaysia by Times Offset (M) Sdn. BHD.

01 00 99 98 97
10 9 8 7 6 5 4 3 2 1

ISBN 0 431 04262 4

British Library Cataloguing in Publication Data

Shuter, Jane
  School. – (Picture the past)
  1. Education – History – Juvenile literature
  2. Schools – History – Juvenile literature
  3. Schools – Pictorial works – Juvenile literature
  I. Title
  370.09

Acknowledgements
The authors and publishers would like to thank the following for permission to use
photographs and other illustrative material:
Banbury Museum/Oxford Photographic Archive, page 16;
Beck Isle Museum, page 4, top;
The Peter Gillies Collection, page 4, bottom;
Greater London Record Office, pages 8, 12;
The Mansell Collection, page 5;
Oxfordshire Photographic Archive, pages 6, 10, 16;
Popperfoto, page 14;
Topham Picturepoint, pages 18, 20.

Cover photographs reproduced with permission of Topham Picturepoint and
Greater London Record Office.

Our thanks to Betty Root for her comments in the preparation of this book.

Contents

Some words are shown in bold text, **like this**. You can find out what these words mean by looking in the glossary on page 24.

Taking photos

People started taking photos in the 1830s. It took over an hour to take a photo! By the 1860s it only took 15 minutes.

When cameras were first invented, they could only take black and white photos. If people wanted colour photos, they had to paint them by hand.

This is one of the earliest photos of a school. It shows a school for poor children in Scotland in 1857. At the time, children did not have to go to school. Most poor children had started work by the age of ten.

Most classrooms were like this one. The children sit at desks, in rows. They face the front of the class, where the teacher and the blackboard are.

The children work on this part of the desk. They have their reading books out.

The children keep the things they are not using on this shelf.

The girls are all wearing **pinafores** to keep their clothes clean.

Can you find
- the blackboard?
- the map?
- the part of the desk where the children put pencils and pens?

Blackheath Elementary School, 1906

The boys in this photo are doing **drill** (PE). They have not changed their clothes for drill.

The classroom was heated by large radiators full of hot water.

The room was lit by gas lamps.

The teacher and the boys wrote in ink. They had to dip their pens in ink pots.

Can you find
- the piano?
- the teacher's desk on its platform?
- where the clock is?

Summertown infant's class, 1910

The children in this photo are making models with clay. They have boards to work on, so they do not get the desks dirty.

The children have been studying flags.

The teacher and the children are in their best clothes for the photo.

Each desk has space for two children.

Can you find
- how the classroom is heated?
- the piano?
- a boy with a big lace collar?

Hackney Downs School, June 1911

The boys in this photo are having a **craft** lesson. They are drawing what they are going to make.

This is a **vice**. It is mostly used to hold things steady.

Everything has to be put away neatly. There are drawers to hold everything.

Each boy is wearing a stiff **collar**. This was part of the **uniform**.

Can you find
- where the wood is kept?
- where the boys hang their jackets?
- the teacher?

A classroom in 1912

By 1912, it was over 30 years since the first law was made saying children had to go to school. Children still sat at desks, in rows, facing the teacher's desk.

This classroom had lots of glass cupboards for putting things on show.

These little **china** pots had ink in them for the children's pens.

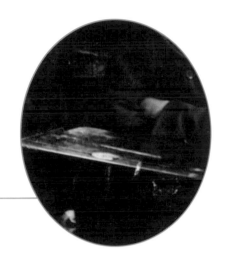

The children learned the names of these shapes.

Can you find

- the teacher's desk?
- a shape the children could draw, hanging on the wall?
- a boy with no jacket, **collar** or tie?

The County School, Banbury, 1920

These boys are having a **craft** lesson.
They are making things from wood.

This is a **plane**. It takes thin strips off the wood to get it to the right shape.

The tools are kept in a rack on the bench.

The boys are making tables. This boy has finished his.

What's different?

Schools were not all the same. Look at the photo on page 12. Think about:

- the **uniforms** the boys are wearing
- the benches and tools they are using.

Deerhurst Village School, 1951

The children in this photo are listening to a radio programme for schools. They are clapping with the music.

The room was heated by a fire. This is the poker used to prod the fire.

The children walked to school in their wellington boots. It was muddy!

The children made pictures on cloth. Here is the cloth they used.

Can you find

- tidied desks and chairs?
- what time of year it is (look at the flowers on the mantelpiece)?
- three pairs of shoes?

School dinners, 1952

These children are having their dinner.
Most children had their main meal in the
middle of the day. Some of them went
home to eat.

Children in aprons take the food from the **serving hatch** to the other children.

Dirty plates are stacked neatly on this trolley.

This teacher has her hat on, ready to go out on playground duty.

Can you find

- the tin for dirty knives and forks?
- a girl with her dinner stuck in her teeth?
- children waiting for their food?
- what the time is?

Did you find?

Beckley Village
School, 1906,
pages 6–7

Blackheath Elementary
School, 1906,
pages 8–9

Summertown
infants class, 1910,
pages 10–11

Hackney Downs School, June 1911, pages 12–13

A classroom in 1912, pages 14–15

Deerhurst Village School, 1951, pages 18–19

School dinners, 1952, pages 20–21

● ten past twelve

Glossary (What words mean)

china baked and painted clay. Cups and plates are often made from china.

collar collars were sold separately from shirts and fixed on with buttons or studs

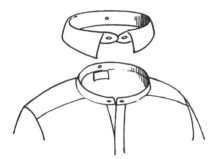

craft making things with your hands

drill PE or group exercises

pinafore an apron

plane a tool which takes thin strips off a piece of wood

serving hatch a hole in the wall between the kitchen and the dining room, with a work-top for trays of food. A hatch slides up and down to open and close the hole.

uniform special clothes that children wear for school so that everyone looks the same

vice a tool which holds things tight

Index